Journaling Through the Seasons
Winter & Word
Bonnie Liabenow

In the heart of winter's silence,
Upon the world so stark and bare,
Lingers a deep and quiet patience,
A muted song of waiting there.

The trees, with limbs outstretched in longing,
Dream of spring's embrace anew,
Frozen streams, their flow suspended,
Yearn for thaw and waters blue.

Snowflakes, each a pause in heaven,
Gently fall, the world to bide,
Heralding a time of waiting,
Nature's rhythm, none can hide.
In the hush of cold, there's promise,
Buried seeds in restful sleep,
Dreaming of the sun's warm kisses,
And the life they're meant to keep.

Cottages with windows frosted,
Inside, flames of fireplaces glow,
Families gather, stories whispered,
Waiting for the melt of snow.
Every pause, each moment's stillness,
In the winter's crisp domain,
Echoes with a timeless yearning,
For life to burst forth once again.

So we wait, with nature's cadence,
For the turn of season's wheel,
In the heart of winter's quiet,
Hope is what we truly feel.

— UNKNOWN

Contents

    Response:
    Take inspiration from these Songs of Worship and
    Praise, and Prayers of Petition and Blessings. Highlight
    words within the songs and prayers that bring a
    meaningful timely message to you. Then write your
    heartfelt response.

    Note from the author:
    Some psalms are my own adaptation, inspired by a particular season I was
    going through, and transformed into my own prayers. I encourage you to
    go through the scripture and read the full psalm.

    Reflection:
    Poems, Quotes, Stories and Prompt Exercises

    Notes:
    What I learned and do not want to forget

"Like the seasons of nature: winter, spring,
summer, and fall – so are the seasons of life.
Seasons are specific periods of time, and they
vary in length. Some seasons last for a period of
years, while others can be just a few short months."
— *Excellence with Simple Elegance*, p. 102

A winter season of life is represented by a pause and is themed,
"In the Waiting."

WAITING, v.

"...to allow time to go by; to delay action until
someone comes, until something that you are
expecting happens or until you can do something."
— CAMBRIDGE DICTIONARY

"Blessed is the man who listens to me. Watching daily at my gates. Waiting at the posts of my doors. For whoever finds me finds life, And obtains favor from the Lord."
– PROVERBS 8:34-35(NKJV)

"With all my heart, I am waiting, Lord, for you! I trust your promises." – PSALM 130:5(CEV)

"Wait patiently for the Lord. Be brave and courageous—He will strengthen your heart; Wait, patiently on the Lord." – PSALM 27:14 (NLT)

"Therefore I will look to the Lord, I will wait for the God of my salvation; my God will hear me." – MICAH 7:7 (NKJV)

WORD, n.

> "...the expressed or manifested mind and will of God." – MERRIAM WEBSTER DICTIONARY

"In the beginning was the Word, and the Word was with God, and the Word was God." – JOHN 1:1 (NIV)

"The Word of our God will stand forever." – ISAIAH 40:8 (ESV)

"So the Word became human and made his home among us. He was full of unfailing love and faithfulness. And we have seen his glory, the glory of the Father's one and only Son." – JOHN 1:14 (NLT)

The *Benefits* of Journaling

Why Journal?

As I look through my past journals, I see how God has been working in my life—and that reminds me that He is constantly present. — BONNIE LIABENOW

THERE'S something about writing – something about jotting down how we've felt and what we've learned in a fleeting moment on a day that may have seemed otherwise unremarkable. We so often remember the grandest core memories – where God's work was so evident, he seemingly all but showed up and shook hands around the room. But when life moves fast, smaller moments move faster, and even the most joyful ones dissipate to join those now forgotten.

Journaling can preserve them. Journaling can capture and preserve the tireless work of God in our everyday lives so that we may reflect, grow and sometimes just find peace in knowing that He's there. Here are some of the benefits you'll notice as you continue this practice:

❄ **Objective Reflection**: Journaling is a factual account of your journey. This helps us take a more objective look at our lives and our progress, helping us realize that we are indeed moving ahead.

❄ **A Safe Space for Emotional Expression**: Journaling provides a private, non-judgmental space for emotional expression and exploration. Your journal is one of the few places you don't have to censor yourself or worry about outside reactions to your thoughts.

❄ **Stress Management**: Journaling can help manage the stress of juggling multiple roles — employee, parent, spouse, caregiver, etc., we have every day. It can help reduce stress by organizing thoughts and problems, making them feel more manageable.

❄ **Self-Awareness**: Journaling regularly can help us become more aware of our thoughts, feelings, and behaviors. This can lead to better self-understanding, growth, and personal development.

❄ **Memory and Cognitive Function**: Journaling can enhance memory and cognitive functions. It encourages the brain to dissect experiences and memories, which can lead to improved comprehension and recall.

❄ **Healing**: Journaling has been used as a tool in therapeutic settings and for self-help, as writing about traumas or negative experiences can help in the healing process.

❄ **Empowerment**: Journaling allows each of us to express our personal experiences, ideas, and views freely. It can be a tool for empowerment, helping each of us find our voice in a society where we may feel unheard.

❄ **Goal Setting and Personal Growth:** Journaling can assist in setting and tracking goals; it can be a great tool for personal growth, helping to monitor progress over time.

HOW WILL THIS HELP ME GROW IN MY FAITH?

When you reflect on how good God is—and all the great things He has done, is doing, and even will do in your life—there's a natural sense of gratefulness. Documenting these moments protects you from ever taking for granted the love and mercy of God in your life—the moments that so quickly fade are great blessings, and they are enough to keep us amazed. — BONNIE LIABENOW

The habit of journaling can strengthen your spiritual walk as it encourages you to dedicate time to your faith, beliefs, and spiritual insights. Your journal allows you to identify what is starving your spirit and brings quietness to a busy day.

WHERE DO I START?

I write down verses that encourage me, some of the prayer requests I'm praying that day, things I feel like the Lord is putting on my heart, and the good things that God does for me. If I want to hear God speak to me, the first thing I do is say, "God, I want you to speak to me. Hearing from you is not just nice, it is a necessity!" And then I withdraw and get alone and quiet. ("Be still and know that I am God.") And then I wait quietly, patiently, and expectantly on God. I ask a specific question, I look into his Word and then when I see God's answer, I write it down. Habakkuk said, "The Lord gave me this answer, 'Write down clearly... what I reveal to you...'" — BONNIE LIABENOW

Choose one of the topics below that resonates most with you. Start small so you don't feel overwhelmed, and take it just one sentence at a time. Length of entry doesn't matter–only your authenticity. You can:

❅ Write about the goodness of God in your life! Write about a tough situation when God has protected and guided you.

❅ Keep a record of your petitions and blessings.

❅ Make it a gratitude journal of your words of praise and worship using the different names for God provided in the prompts given.

Not every day will look the same, and that's welcomed and expected.

TIPS FOR JOURNALING

❅ **Redefine journaling.** This is not the same as keeping a diary. A diary is, 'Dear diary, this is what I did today.' A journal is, 'This is what I learned today.'

❅ **Write spiritual encounters.** If it's on your heart, don't hesitate to write it down. All spiritual encounters with the most Holy God are worthy of documenting.

❅ **Write your heartfelt response.** Start by reading scripture (each psalm) two or three times with the prayerful question in mind: *What does God want me to hear, read, or see from this? How does this resonate with me? As I meditate on the words, what stands out? Does it provide answers? Does it raise questions? Or does it not resonate at all, and why?* Ask God for clarity in these lines.

❅ **Same time.** Set a time each day to sit and self-reflect on your journey. You may look at how you are feeling and examine why you feel that way. You can also write down things that inspire you throughout the day.

❈ **Read for inspiration.** Reading your daily writing can help you work toward new goals, search for more answers to questions you've had in the last month, and give thanks for the lessons you've already learned.

❈ **Set goals.** Setting goals can inspire you. These can be things you wish to do on a daily basis to further your personal growth or things you hope to do within a certain amount of time. Refer to *Excellence with Simple Elegance, Chapter: Goal Setting, Page 145* and also *The Study* for more guidance.

❈ **Practice gratitude.** It helps to create a thankful heart. Acknowledge your blessings. Write about the things in your day that make you feel grateful. Research shows that people who make a point to feel gratitude are happier and healthier people.

❈ **Document.** Write down accounts in which you see God working in your life like answers to prayers, and God's favor and blessings given to you. Journaling brings awareness of God's presence in our life, especially that God shows up in both Big ways and small blessings.

❈ **Take it with you.** Keep your journal with you at all times. Keeping your journal on hand allows you to write down quotes, spiritual text references, or general thoughts you wish to reflect on right when they come to mind.

❈ **Look back.** Review your journal entries at least once a month. By taking time to self-reflect on your prior entries, you can better see the direction you're heading in spiritual enlightenment.

❄ **Be authentic.** The Book of Psalms is a great example of journal writing. David took the first five books of the Bible: Genesis, Exodus, Leviticus, Numbers, Deuteronomy, and he meditated on them day and night and wrote his prayers down. As you read the Psalms, you'll see that David includes just about every emotion known to the human race including envy, jealousy, lust, and greed. David is brutally honest in his writing; he does not write what he thinks, he writes what he honestly feels. This paves a path of authenticity, setting a powerful example for us in our own journaling.

❄ **Enjoy It.**

A Note on *Winter* and *Waiting*

By Meghan Dryzga

> *And the world was quiet.*
>
> *No purr of engines through the streets.*
>
> *No chorus of children in the yard.*
>
> *Even the wind wouldn't dare*
>
> *scare the air into howling.*
>
> *And as the snow floated down*
>
> *I was surprised to find it had a sound*
>
> *that had been, until now, drowned*
>
> *out by the world when it was moving.*

Do you remember the waiting? Day after day we ached for the restoration of lives we'd known – lives we'd grown accustomed to: The busy, the bustle, the hundreds of daily human connections we didn't realize we were taking for granted. When the world saw its 2020 diagnosis, life came to a screeching halt. At least, it seemed. And I waited for life to resume, frustrated and fidgeting, like I was watching an unwrapped present before the sun crests over the horizon on Christmas morning.

And I waited. And waited.

And the world remained unmoving in its long winter's nap.

But then, slowly, it was as if God brewed a cup of coffee, and the fragrance began to swell, awakening a hunger for more than just the *waiting*. See, somewhere in the stillness of that winter season, the world became so quiet, it was as if I could hear the hands of God begin to work. He gifted me time—swaths of time previously usurped by a nine-to-five job and after-school activities—and a sudden hunger to fill the minutes with great intention.

Each day, I began connecting with voices from seasoned friendships I'd longed to hear for years.

Each day, I began connecting with my husband on walks we hadn't taken time for in a decade.

Each day, I began connecting with my children over more than the dinner menu and geometry; I coached my children on real-life circumstances they'll draw from for years.

What a winter. What an opportunity, disguised. What a time to transform waiting into a fruit-bearing season.

In this journal, Bonnie positions us to dive deep into those moments when we are still and waiting so that we may discover who we have the potential to become. How might we serve a purpose that may not be immediately apparent? What intentions of our own are blocking us from seeing His plans?

When the world stopped churning, I was presented with an invaluable gift that I couldn't see at first. it was only discovered by being still and fighting the inclination to wish away the whole season.

I am not alone. When Bonnie traversed the topics of winter and waiting with women in her network, so many seemed to have their own story of unexpected self-discovery. In the reflections ahead, you'll hear some of these stories and perspectives from Mary Kathleen, Rosie, Nancy and Kim. Sit with them and listen for connections that resonate with your experiences. Then be still in your most blustery winter seasons, remember those stories, and listen for the crunch of snow beneath His heels as He guides you toward a path, unexpected, like in the anecdotes you'll read here.

You know, there's a social media trend of thousands of video posts with lyrics singing, "Let's skip to the good part…" The reels capture a before-and-after story where the "before" shows the author without something they desire; when the lyrics call out, "let's skip to the good part," the video cuts to the author now in possession of that anticipated, desired thing. The *waiting* between "before" and "after" is, of course, not represented in the videos.

It's dreamy to think of life's toughest seasons going this way—when we just skip ahead to the solution we so desire. But what would we miss? Perhaps we learn in the waiting that the initial desired outcome wasn't a fitting outcome for our story (Nancy). Perhaps we learn we're needed more somewhere else. Or that our desired outcome doesn't have the value we imagined (Rosie). Or maybe, that our perception of the silence wasn't at all the reality (Kim). The value between before and after is the listening and learning that reveal God's purpose for us—beyond our forced, desired outcomes. When we listen, He guides us on a path of His intentions. As much as we may want to at first, resist the temptation to wish away the waiting and skip to the good part. There's a reward in the silence if you know what to listen for.

And as the snow floated down,

I was surprised to find it had a sound.

Peaceful in its own descent,

Damping thoughts of my intent,

Filling in the prints I'd pressed.

Waiting seemed a fruitless step.

Silent, glistening, humble snow —

This way now; be still and know.

A Winter Song of *Worship* and *Praise*

Inspired By Psalm 3, 22, & 29

Jehovah-Kobodhi — Lord my Glory

I will be faithful to honor You, Lord, for the glory of Your name. In the splendor of Your holiness, I will fall down and worship You. O Lord, be close to me. O my Strength, save my life for You are faithful to answer me. Salvation belongs to You alone for Your blessing is upon me. You shield me.

You are the One who lifts up my head when I do not have the strength. O Lord, my Glory!

I will praise You. I fear You and will give You all my praise. I will honor You and fear You, for You have not turned away from my suffering or trouble. You have heard my cry. My praise will be from You. I will keep my promises.

May Your heart live forever O Lord, my Glory!

All the ends of the earth will remember and turn to You. All the families of the nations will worship before You. For the holy nation is Yours, and You rule over all the nations. All the proud ones of the earth will worship. All who go down to the dust will fall to their knees before You, even those who cannot keep their soul alive. Future children will serve You, and they will tell of Your greatness to their children. They will tell of Your saving power to people who are yet to be born. Your mighty voice echoes above the sea. Your voice is powerful and majestic. Your voice strikes with bolts of lightning as You rule over the floodwaters.

In all Your glory, You reign as King forever.

A Winter Song of
Worship AND *Praise*

Highlight and respond below

Inspired By Psalm 3, 22, & 29

Jehovah-Kobodhi - Lord my Glory

____

____

____

____

I WILL be faithful to honor You, Lord, for the glory of Your name. In the splendor of Your holiness, I will fall down and worship You. O Lord, be close to me. O my Strength, save my life for You are faithful to answer me. Salvation belongs to You alone for Your blessing is upon me. You shield me.

____

____

____

____

You are the One who lifts up my head when I do not have the strength. O Lord, my Glory!

I will praise You. I fear You and will give You all my praise. I will honor You and fear You, for You have not turned away from my suffering or trouble. You have heard my cry. My praise will be from You. I will keep my promises.

May Your heart live forever O Lord, my Glory!

All the ends of the earth will remember and turn to You. All the families of the nations will worship before You. For the holy nation is Yours, and You rule over all the nations. All the proud ones of the earth will worship. All who go down to the dust will fall to their knees before You, even those who cannot keep their soul alive. Future children will serve You, and they will tell of Your greatness to their children. They will tell of Your saving power to people who are yet to be born. Your mighty voice echoes above the sea. Your voice is powerful and majestic. Your voice strikes with bolts of lightning as You rule over the floodwaters.

In all Your glory, You reign as King forever.

Reflection:

"Every winter, I am reminded that this is a time for deep intimacy with my thoughts. Activity gives way to a more dormant life out of the cold. This is truly a time for introspection, introversion and contemplation. A quiet mind and soul allows for me to reflect on the year I just lived. An outpouring of new questions arises, and opportunities are within reach. It is all a matter of my decision to take the steps to seize the moments that lay in front of me. A new calendar year is upon me, begging me to accept a new journey. The question is, 'How focused am I to allow God to take control of this season so that I become aware of the things He needs me to see and learn from?'" — MARY KATHLEEN

Self Awareness:

As you reflect on past winter seasons of life, have you taken time for deep intimacy with your thoughts? Reflect and write some of the intimate thoughts in the snowflakes below.

During a time for introspection, introversion and contempla-tion, what are the hard lessons that you were grateful to learn? Write of these lessons in the snowflakes below.

Are you focused on allowing God to take control of this season so that you become aware of the things He needs you to see and learn from?

How do you need to change your daily routines so you are aware of God's leading and guidance? Write in the snowflakes below.

What are the next steps you'll consider to give way to an unshakeable faith that will lead the next generation? Write in the snowflakes below.

Notes

Notes

Notes

Notes

A Winter Prayer of
Petition AND *Blessing*

Inspired By Psalm 10 & 90

Jehovah—Helech 'Olam- God Is Forever

Rise up, O Lord! Lift up Your hand, O God. Do not forget me. You have heard my prayers. Give strength to my heart and listen to my petition. For You, O Lord, are King forever and ever.

Lord, You have been the place of comfort for me. Before the mountains were born, before You gave birth to the earth and the world, forever and ever, You were God. A thousand years in Your eyes are like yesterday or like the hours of the night.

You know my sin and have set each wrongdoing before You. My secret sins are illuminated in the light of Your face. All my days pass away in the midst of Your anger. I will finish my years with a quiet cry. The days of my life are short, maybe seventy or eighty if I have the strength to carry on. Sometimes it seems the best of my days are only hard work and sorrow. Oh, how I long for Your mercy and forgiveness.

Rise up, O Lord! Lift up Your hand, O God. Do not forget me. You have heard my prayers. Give strength to my heart and listen to my petitions. For You, O Lord, are King forever and ever.

Teach me to understand. Give me a heart of wisdom so that I may give back to You. Teach me to live well so I may experience happiness. Teach me to live wisely! Surprise me with Your love each morning so I may skip and dance all the day long. Let me see Your best works and the ways You rule and bless Your children. Let Your loveliness rest on me, confirming Your work in me. Each day I long to experience Your greatness and Your favor. For you, O Lord, are King forever and ever. Amen.

A Winter Prayer of
Petition AND *Blessing*

Highlight and respond below

Inspired By Psalm 10 & 90

Jehovah—Helech 'Olam – God Is Forever

____

____

____

____

____

RISE up, O Lord! Lift up Your hand, O God. Do not forget me. You have heard my prayers. Give strength to my heart and listen to my petition. For You, O Lord, are King forever and ever.

____

____

____

____

____

Lord, You have been the place of comfort for me. Before the mountains were born, before You gave birth to the earth and the world, forever and ever, You were God. A thousand years in Your eyes are like yesterday or like the hours of the night.

You know my sin and have set each wrongdoing before You. My secret sins are illuminated in the light of Your face. All my days pass away in the midst of Your anger. I will finish my years with a quiet cry. The days of my life are short, maybe seventy or eighty if I have the strength to carry on. Sometimes it seems the best of my days are only hard work and sorrow. Oh, how I long for Your mercy and forgiveness.

Rise up, O Lord! Lift up Your hand, O God. Do not forget me. You have heard my prayers. Give strength to my heart and listen to my petitions. For You, O Lord, are King forever and ever.

Teach me to understand. Give me a heart of wisdom so that I may give back to You. Teach me to live well so I may experience happiness. Teach me to live wisely! Surprise me with Your love each morning so I may skip and dance all the day long. Let me see Your best works and the ways You rule and bless Your children. Let Your loveliness rest on me, confirming Your work in me. Each day I long to experience Your greatness and Your favor. For you, O Lord, are King forever and ever. Amen.

Reflection:

"Rest is not idle, is not wasteful. Sometimes rest is the most productive thing you can do for body and soul." — ERICA LAYNE

Stress Management:

According to the Mayo Clinic Health System, adequate quality rest is essential for good health. Rest is vital for better mental health, increased concentration and memory, a healthier immune system, reduced stress, improved mood and even a better metabolism. If rest is the most productive thing we can do for the soul and body, what does rest look like for you? Choose and circle.

❋ 8 hours of sleeping, nightly	❋ Praying
❋ Quietly Sitting	❋ Listening to music
❋ Reading	❋ Sundays once a week
❋ Walking or Running	❋ Coffee time
❋ Dreaming	❋ Writing

Place your chosen method of rest in each of the 4 parts given below. Write how this method will bring you the type of rest listed during a season of waiting. Then, commit to implementing a routine of care for yourself.

Spiritual: _______________________________

____

____

____

____

____

Emotional: _______________________________

____

____

____

____

____

Mental: _______________________________

____

____

____

____

____

Physical

____

____

____

____

____

____

Many times, identifying what or who has recently caused you the most overwhelm is the first step to embracing a period of rest. Write the story.

____

____

____

____

____

____

Who or what could support you the most right now in this time of rest? How will you recruit this support?

____

____

____

____

____

Notes

Notes

Notes

Notes

A Winter Prayer of *Petition* and *Blessing*

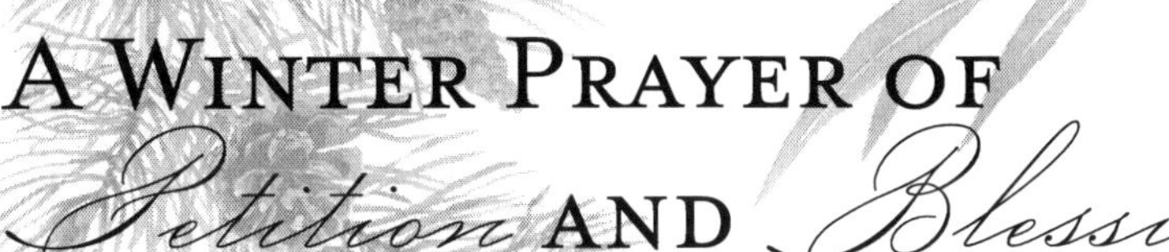

Inspired By Psalm 82, 83 & 94

Jehovah-Hashopet — Lord my Judge

"The Lord is the Judge. May He decide today" — Judges 11:27

O Lord, the God Who punishes, let Your light shine!

God, put an end to evil; please show Your colors! Judge the earth and take Your stand. The evil that comes against me daily surely overwhelms me. As for the wicked, God, they brag and boast. They walk all over Your people. God, they abuse Your precious people. They take out anyone who gets in their way. They know nothing and understand nothing. They walk around in the dark. Do the right thing for the weak and those without a father. Stand up for the rights of those who are suffering and in need. Save the weak and those in need. Set them free from the hand of the sinful.

Rise up, O God! Say who is guilty or not guilty upon the earth! For all the nations belong to You.

O God, do not keep quiet. Do not hold Your peace. See those who hate You and make much noise. Those who fight against You have honored themselves. They make bad plans against Your people. They plan against those for whom You care. They plan together with one mind and make an agreement against You.

O Lord, the God Who punishes, let Your light shine! God, put an end to evil; please show Your colors! Judge of the earth, take Your stand.

A Winter Prayer of
Petition AND *Blessing*

Highlight and respond below

Inspired By Psalm 82, 83 & 94

Jehovah-Hashopet — Lord my Judge

____

____

____

"The Lord is the Judge. May He decide today" — Judges 11:27

____

____

____

____

O Lord, the God Who punishes, let Your light shine!

____

____

____

____

God, put an end to evil; please show Your colors! Judge the earth and take Your stand. The evil that comes against me daily surely overwhelms me. As for the wicked, God, they brag and boast. They walk all over Your people. God, they abuse Your precious people. They take out anyone who gets in their way. They know nothing and understand nothing. They walk around in the dark. Do the right thing for the weak and those without a father. Stand up for the rights of those who are suffering and in need. Save the weak and those in need. Set them free from the hand of the sinful.

____

____

____

____

____

____

____

____

Rise up, O God! Say who is guilty or not guilty upon the earth! For all the nations belong to You.

____

____

____

____

____

O God, do not keep quiet. Do not hold Your peace. See those who hate You and make much noise. Those who fight against You have honored themselves. They make bad plans against Your people. They plan against those for whom You care. They plan together with one mind and make an agreement against You.

O Lord, the God Who punishes, let Your light shine! God, put an end to evil; please show Your colors! Judge of the earth, take Your stand.

Reflection:

"Until God is enough, nothing else will be." — TOBY MAC

I felt unsettled, sick and worried about the future. Next came a period of introspection and discipline, devotion, meditation, physical training, a strict diet and isolation outside of work. This helped me focus and plan the next steps in my life.

I came to grips with the reality of being alone. I surrounded myself with a group I called my "private board of directors" – people who would give me sound advice backed by wisdom and life experience. These people cannot be compromised and, although it wasn't required, each of them is a strong believer.

I blocked out the white noise of my past life and asked for God's will in my life, now. I set boundaries with my family. I deliberately disengaged from social situations that weren't healthy for me. I started caring about what God thought instead of what anyone else thought. Controlling who I listened to and what I absorbed changed my life perspective. Even now, I have zero televisions in my home.

Just when I thought I'd climbed the mountain, I was in a nearly tragic motorcycle accident. My faith grew stronger as angel paramedics, trauma nurses and surgeons saved me. At 53 years old, I realized God didn't promise us a problem-free life. He promised to be a light in the dark, and He delivers every time if we ask.

Psalm 23:1-3 is literal for me:

The Lord is my shepherd.

I ask Him every day for his will in my life. And I study his Word.

I shall not be in want

He has met all of my needs, including needs I didn't even realize I had.

He makes me lie down in green pastures.

I am no longer a manic "doer"; I've learned the importance of rest and reflection and find myself more productive.

He leads me beside quiet waters.

Much of my downtime is spent on a paddle board, a pontoon boat or watching the lake from my cottage.

He restores my soul.

I'm no longer a broken perfectionist. The Lord rebuilt me physically, mentally, emotionally and spiritually.

He guides me in paths of righteousness for His name's sake.

Since this transformation, I've had individuals reach out in desperate times for help. I listen to them first and then ask for God's help with my response to comfort and guide them. I've also been able to help non-profit agencies stay solvent with God's help.

Running parallel in my journey is the realization that everything happens on God's timeline. It's not ours to question. If we live life with love, gratitude, acceptance and patience, we are walking in faith. I never thought that my life would look like this, and I've never felt this much joy. I've got the peace that passes understanding. Praise the Lord! — KATY

Personal Growth:

Tell the story of key moments in your spiritual journey from childhood to today. Include memorable moments among the history of your family and your experiences growing up.

____

____

____

____

____

____

How do you discern the presence of God in your life, and how does His Word guide you?

_____________________   _____________________

_____________________   _____________________

What are your predominant feelings about your relationship with God?

_____________________   _____________________

_____________________   _____________________

What is your desire for God?

_____________________________   _____________________________

_____________________________   _____________________________

What is God's desire for you?

_____________________________   _____________________________

_____________________________   _____________________________

Write a prayer asking God to bring a new awareness of His presence in your life.

____

____

____

____

____

____

Notes

Notes

Notes

A WINTER SONG OF *Worship* AND *Praise*

INSPIRED BY PSALM 30, 34 & 111

Jehovah–Metshodhathi – Lord my Fortress

The Lord Be Praised

Praise You, O Lord! In worship, I will give thanks to You with all my heart. Your works are great. I find great joy to be in Your house. There, I have witnessed the great and powerful work of Your loving hand. You have met me there. I have felt Your presence. You are right and good and forever. Your great works will never be erased from my memory. I will remember how You show loving favor and compassion. I hold dear to Your promises. They are forever. I look to You for daily guidance, pouring out my petitions, and You never fail me. You answer me. You take away all my fears and cause my face to shine with joy.

You have turned my crying into dancing. You have dressed me with joy so my soul may sing praise to You and not be quiet. O Lord, my God, I will give thanks to You forever. I will honor You at all times. Your praise will always be in my mouth. My soul will be proud to tell about You. I will exalt You for You rescued me. I cried to You for help, and You restored my health. I will sing to You and praise Your holy name. For Your anger lasts only a moment, but Your favor lasts a lifetime!

As for me, I will never be moved. O Lord, by Your favor, You have made my mountain strong. Weeping may last through the night, but joy comes with the morning.

Praise You Lord! O taste and see that You are good. The works of Your hands are faithful and right. Your Laws and promises are true. They stand strong forever and ever. You have made a way for Your people to be free. Your holy name is to be honored with fear. To fear You is the beginning of wisdom. Happy is the one who trusts in You! For those who fear You never want for anything and Your eyes are on those who do what is right and good. Your ears are open to their cry. You hear them and take them from all their troubles. You are near to those who have a broken heart and save those who are broken in spirit. May Your people keep their tongues from sin and their lips from speaking lies. May Your people turn away from what is sinful and do what is good. May they look for peace and follow it.

You have turned my crying into dancing. You have dressed me with joy so my soul may sing praise to You and not be quiet. O Lord my God, I will give thanks to You forever. I will honor You at all times. Your praise will always be in my mouth. My soul will be proud to tell about You. I will exalt you, Lord, for You rescued me. I cried to You for help, and You restored my health. I will sing to You and praise Your holy name. For Your anger lasts only a moment, but Your favor lasts a lifetime!

As for me, I will never be moved. O Lord, by Your favor, You have made my mountain strong. Weeping may last through the night, but joy comes with the morning.

A Winter Song of
Worship AND *Praise*

Highlight and respond below

INSPIRED BY PSALM 30, 34 & 111

Jehovah–Metshodhathi — Lord my Fortress

____

____

____

____

____

THE Lord Be Praised

____

____

____

____

____

____

Praise You, O Lord! In worship, I will give thanks to You with all my heart. Your works are great. I find great joy to be in Your house. There, I have witnessed the great and powerful work of Your loving hand. You have met me there. I have felt Your presence. You are right and good and forever. Your great works will never be erased from my memory. I will remember how You show loving favor and compassion. I hold dear to Your promises. They are forever. I look to You for daily guidance, pouring out my petitions, and You never fail me. You answer me. You take away all my fears and cause my face to shine with joy.

____

____

____

____

____

You have turned my crying into dancing. You have dressed me with joy so my soul may sing praise to You and not be quiet. O Lord, my God, I will give thanks to You forever. I will honor You at all times. Your praise will always be in my mouth. My soul will be proud to tell about You. I will exalt You for You rescued me. I cried to You for help, and You restored my health. I will sing to You and praise Your holy name. For Your anger lasts only a moment, but Your favor lasts a lifetime!

____

____

____

____

As for me, I will never be moved. O Lord, by Your favor, You have made my mountain strong. Weeping may last through the night, but joy comes with the morning.

Praise You Lord! O taste and see that You are good. The works of Your hands are faithful and right. Your Laws and promises are true. They stand strong forever and ever. You have made a way for Your people to be free. Your holy name is to be honored with fear. To fear You is the beginning of wisdom. Happy is the one who trusts in You! For those who fear You never want for anything and Your eyes are on those who do what is right and good. Your ears are open to their cry. You hear them and take them from all their troubles. You are near to those who have a broken heart and save those who are broken in spirit. May Your people keep their tongues from sin and their lips from speaking lies. May Your people turn away from what is sinful and do what is good. May they look for peace and follow it.

You have turned my crying into dancing. You have dressed me with joy so my soul may sing praise to You and not be quiet. O Lord my God, I will give thanks to You forever. I will honor You at all times. Your praise will always be in my mouth. My soul will be proud to tell about You. I will exalt you, Lord, for You rescued me. I cried to You for help, and You restored my health. I will sing to You and praise Your holy name. For Your anger lasts only a moment, but Your favor lasts a lifetime!

As for me, I will never be moved. O Lord, by Your favor, You have made my mountain strong. Weeping may last through the night, but joy comes with the morning.

Reflection:

"Snowfall rouses your inner child to dream and play once more."
— Angie Weiland Crosby

Memory and Cognition:

Reflect on a childhood memory that included a delightful activity which brought tons of joy. Write in the snowflakes.

Be intentional about returning play and enjoyment to every day. Begin by remembering the good. What was your favorite thing about today?

What makes you laugh and smile?

Notes

Notes

Notes

A WINTER PRAYER OF *Petition* AND *Blessing*

INSPIRED BY PSALM 91 & 57

Jehovah–Machsi – The Lord, who is my refuge

He who lives in the safe place of the Most High will be in the shadow of the All-powerful, the One I Trust.

Show me loving kindness, O God. For my soul runs to You where I will be safe in the shadow of Your wings. I will cry to You, O God Most High, You, Who finishes all things for me. You, Who reaches from heaven to save me. You will send Your truth and loving kindness.

O Lord, You are my safe and strong place. You are my God, the One I trust. You will cover me with Your wings. And under Your wings You promise that I will be safe.

God, I know you are faithful like a safe covering and a strong wall. I will not be afraid of trouble at night, or of the arrow that flies by day. I will not be afraid of the sickness that walks in darkness, or of the trouble that destroys at noon. A thousand may fall at my side and ten thousand at my right hand. But trouble will not come near me because I have made You my safe place, and the place where I live, nothing will hurt me. No trouble will come near my home. You will please me with a long life and show favor that I may see Your saving power.

Be lifted up above the heavens, O God. Let Your shining greatness be above all the earth and reveal to me Your saving power, for You are the One I trust.

I have known Your heavenly name and will call upon You. You will reveal to me Your saving power. O God, You will tell Your angels to care for me and keep me in all my ways. Your angels will hold me up in their hands so my foot will not hit against anything harsh. You will bring me out of trouble and set me in a safe place on high. You will please me with a long life and show favor to me. You will be with me in my struggle.

My heart will not be moved, O God. My heart cannot be moved. I will sing, yes, I will sing praises! Awaken, my shining greatness. Awaken, harps. I will rise early in the morning. I'm thanking you, God, out loud in the streets, singing Your praises in town and country. The deeper Your love, the higher it goes; every cloud is a flag to Your faithfulness. Soar high in the skies, O God! Cover the whole earth with Your glory! For Your loving-kindness is great to the heavens and Your truth to the clouds.

O Lord, You are my safe and strong place. You are my God, the One I trust. You will cover me with Your wings. And under Your wings You promise that I will be safe.

A Winter Prayer of
Petition AND *Blessing*

Highlight and respond below

Inspired By Psalm 91 & 57

Jehovah-Machsi - The Lord, who is my refuge

____

____

____

____

____

____

He who lives in the safe place of the Most High will be in the
shadow of the All-powerful, the One I Trust.

____

____

____

____

____

____

Show me loving kindness, O God. For my soul runs to You where I will be safe in the shadow of Your wings. I will cry to You, O God Most High, You, Who finishes all things for me. You, Who reaches from heaven to save me. You will send Your truth and loving kindness.

O Lord, You are my safe and strong place. You are my God, the One I trust. You will cover me with Your wings. And under Your wings You promise that I will be safe.

God, I know you are faithful like a safe covering and a strong wall. I will not be afraid of trouble at night, or of the arrow that flies by day. I will not be afraid of the sickness that walks in darkness, or of the trouble that destroys at noon. A thousand may fall at my side and ten thousand at my right hand. But trouble will not come near me because I have made You my safe place, and the place where I live, nothing will hurt me. No trouble will come near my home. You will please me with a long life and show favor that I may see Your saving power.

Be lifted up above the heavens, O God. Let Your shining greatness be above all the earth and reveal to me Your saving power, for You are the One I trust.

I have known Your heavenly name and will call upon You. You will reveal to me Your saving power. O God, You will tell Your angels to care for me and keep me in all my ways. Your angels will hold me up in their hands so my foot will not hit against anything harsh. You will bring me out of trouble and set me in a safe place on high. You will please me with a long life and show favor to me. You will be with me in my struggle.

____

____

____

____

____

____

My heart will not be moved, O God. My heart cannot be moved. I will sing, yes, I will sing praises! Awaken, my shining greatness. Awaken, harps. I will rise early in the morning. I'm thanking you, God, out loud in the streets, singing Your praises in town and country. The deeper Your love, the higher it goes; every cloud is a flag to Your faithfulness. Soar high in the skies, O God! Cover the whole earth with Your glory! For Your loving-kindness is great to the heavens and Your truth to the clouds.

____

____

____

____

O Lord, You are my safe and strong place. You are my God, the One I trust. You will cover me with Your wings. And under Your wings You promise that I will be safe.

Reflection:

"Remember to take some quiet time to rest, breathe, and listen to the whispers of your heart." — JANE LEE LOGAN

Emotional Expression:

Rest, breathe and listen to the whispers of your heart. What does your heart long for? Circle the responses that resonate with you, or fill in your own.

Happiness	Hope	Time
Contentment	Joy	Restoration
Peace	Stability	Health

______________   ______________   ______________

______________   ______________   ______________

When you envision a future version of yourself that seems happy and aligned with your purpose, how does that look?

____

____

____

____

____

____

____

____

What's going on
in your life that
could get in the
way of that
possibility?

What's distracting
you or making
you feel the
opposite of how
you want to feel?

What steps of obedience is God calling you to that you are avoiding?

List your gifts, talents and passions.

____

____

____

Based on the list of gifts/talents/passions you made above, what do you believe/know is your calling? What manageable, actionable steps can you start taking today to fulfill those whispers of your heart?

____

____

____

Write out a verse or verses from God's Word that will speak to your heart every day and that touches the essence of your heart's whispers.

____

____

____

Notes

Notes

Notes

Notes

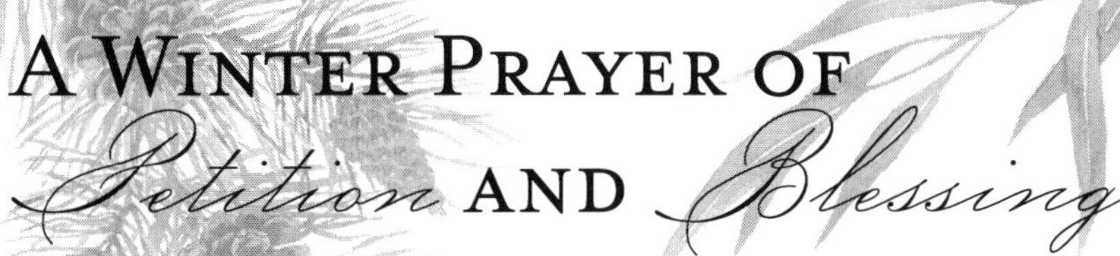

A WINTER PRAYER OF *Petition* AND *Blessing*

INSPIRED BY PSALM 102 & 38

Jehovah–'Uzam–The Lord is my strength in times of trouble

A Prayer Of Faith

"That I, the Lord, am your Savior, And your Redeemer " — Is. 49:26

Please hear my prayer, O Lord! Let my cry for help reach You. Do not hide Your face from me in my moment of trouble. Please listen and hurry to answer me. The days have disappeared and my body has lost life. My heart is crushed and I have forgotten to eat. I am nothing but skin and bones. Hear my loud cries; I am praying, yearning for You to hear me. I lie awake and feel so alone.

Why can't You just hear me and answer my cry? God, I need You to steady my heart. Do not leave me alone, O Lord! Do not be far from me! Hurry to help me, O Lord, the One Who saves me! For I hope in You, O Lord, and I know You will answer.

O Lord, do not speak sharp words to me. Do not punish me. Truly there is no strength in my bones because of my sin. For my sins are gone over my head. Like a heavy load, they weigh too much for me. I cannot stand straight and keep my head down. I have been grieving all day long because my body is filled with burning pain. There is no strength in my body. I am weak and broken. I cry because of the pain in my heart. Lord, all my desire is before You. My breathing from deep within is not hidden from You. My heart beats fast. My strength leaves me. Even the light of my eyes has left me. My loved ones and my friends stay away from me. And I feel so alone.

Why can't You just hear me and answer my cry? God, I need You to steady my heart. Do not leave me alone, O Lord! Do not be far from me! Hurry to help me, O Lord, the One Who saves me! For I hope in You, O Lord, and I know You will answer.

Yet you, God, are sovereign still, always and ever sovereign. You will rise up and show favor to me. I will fear Your name and Your shining greatness. You will answer my prayer and meet my needs. You will not turn from me. I will give thanks for Your faithfulness. It's Your compassion I long to feel. I want to see Your glory. My desire is to worship Your name and give You praise even in this painful time. Truly You have sovereignly brought me to my knees. You are always the same. Your years will never end. The children of those who serve You will live on. And their children will be set before You.

A Winter Prayer of
Petition AND *Blessing*

Highlight and respond below

Inspired By Psalm 102 & 38

Jehovah-'Uzam - The Lord is my strength in times of trouble

A Prayer of Faith

____

____

____

____

____

"That I, the Lord, am your Savior, And your Redeemer" — Is. 49:26

____

____

____

____

____

PLEASE hear my prayer, O Lord! Let my cry for help reach You. Do not hide Your face from me in my moment of trouble. Please listen and hurry to answer me. The days have disappeared and my body has lost life. My heart is crushed and I have forgotten to eat. I am nothing but skin and bones. Hear my loud cries; I am praying, yearning for You to hear me. I lie awake and feel so alone.

____

____

____

____

____

____

Why can't You just hear me and answer my cry? God, I need You to steady my heart. Do not leave me alone, O Lord! Do not be far from me! Hurry to help me, O Lord, the One Who saves me! For I hope in You, O Lord, and I know You will answer.

____

____

____

____

____

____

O Lord, do not speak sharp words to me. Do not punish me. Truly there is no strength in my bones because of my sin. For my sins are gone over my head. Like a heavy load, they weigh too much for me. I cannot stand straight and keep my head down. I have been grieving all day long because my body is filled with burning pain. There is no strength in my body. I am weak and broken. I cry because of the pain in my heart. Lord, all my desire is before You. My breathing from deep within is not hidden from You. My heart beats fast. My strength leaves me. Even the light of my eyes has left me. My loved ones and my friends stay away from me. And I feel so alone.

____

____

____

____

____

____

Why can't You just hear me and answer my cry? God, I need You to steady my heart. Do not leave me alone, O Lord! Do not be far from me! Hurry to help me, O Lord, the One Who saves me! For I hope in You, O Lord, and I know You will answer.

____

____

____

____

____

____

Yet you, God, are sovereign still, always and ever sovereign. You will rise up and show favor to me. I will fear Your name and Your shining greatness. You will answer my prayer and meet my needs. You will not turn from me. I will give thanks for Your faithfulness. It's Your compassion I long to feel. I want to see Your glory. My desire is to worship Your name and give You praise even in this painful time. Truly You have sovereignly brought me to my knees. You are always the same. Your years will never end. The children of those who serve You will live on. And their children will be set before You.

Reflection:

"A gentle reminder: Those heavy bags you're carry-
ing never belonged to you. It's okay to set them down."
—Jane Lee Logan

At that time, I prayed a million prayers, and I questioned if God really hears or cares or wants to help me. My mother was never healed from bi-polar disorder. She was unpredictable, angry, paranoid, and unable to be a "great" mom. I felt alone without her words and wisdom to guide and empower me. But, in the waiting for an answered prayer, I saw glimpses of a gentle woman, a creative soul and a woman with a great memory – even for the foreign language she briefly studied in college.

Soon, I learned to trust that my life of waiting is half a breath in the realm of eternity. I learned that healing can happen on Earth and in Heaven, that God is patient and I needed his eternal outlook. These were the heavy suitcases I could set down to embrace sentiments of forgiveness, deep love, and restoration for both my mother and I. It happens for all His followers, and I know God has healed my mother today in heaven. No tears of sadness. Only reunions of people loved and restored. –Nancy

Healing:

What feels heavy in your life right now?

__________________________ __________________________

__________________________ __________________________

__________________________ __________________________

__________________________ __________________________

Why do you feel you need to carry the things weighing you down?

_______________________ _______________________

_______________________ _______________________

_______________________ _______________________

_______________________ _______________________

What's stopping you from setting them down? Are there times when you're getting in your own way? Does pride or ego get in the way?

____

____

____

____

____

Which heavy things are out of your control?

_______________________ _______________________

_______________________ _______________________

_______________________ _______________________

_______________________ _______________________

Is the weight of carrying these thoughts doing more harm than good? Explain.

____

____

____

____

If you let go of
these negative
thoughts,
what positivity
can you make
room for?

____

____

____

____

____

____

____

____

In light of what you wrote above, write a letter to God asking
Him to captivate your thoughts and emotions around the things
that feel heavy. Then, intentionally surrender them to Him.

____

____

____

____

____

____

____

____

Notes

Notes

Notes

A WINTER SONG OF *Worship* AND *Praise*

INSPIRED BY PSALM 47, 75 & 76

Call out to God with the voice of joy for He is near. God says, "At the time I have planned, I will bring justice. When the earth quakes and its people live in turmoil, I am the One Who keeps its foundations firm."

Sing praises to God. Sing praises. Sing praises to our King. Sing praises. For God is the King of all the earth. Sing praises with a well-written song. God rules over the nations. God sits on His holy throne. Call out to God with the voice of praise for He is near.

I will always proclaim what God has done; I will sing praises to the God of Jacob. I will tell of His wonderful deeds because He stands up to judge and to rescue the oppressed of the earth. I will make my promises to the Lord my God, and I will keep them.

Let everyone bring tribute to the Awesome One. People everywhere tell of His wonderful deeds for He is near. God is honored. He is more glorious and majestic than the everlasting mountains. No wonder He is greatly feared! The earth trembles and stands silent before Him. Many leaders will rise and fall but the Lord is forever.

Show your happiness, friends! How happy is the one whose wrongdoing is forgiven and whose sin is covered! How happy is the one whose sin the Lord does not hold against them and in whose spirit there is nothing false. For the Lord Most High is to be feared. He is a great King over all the earth. God has gone up with a loud voice and with the sound of a horn.

Sing praises to God. Sing praises. Sing praises to our King. Sing praises. For God is the King of all the earth. Sing praises with a well-written song. God rules over the nations. God sits on His holy throne. Call out to God with a voice of praise for He is near.

I lift up my hands to His holy place. May honor and thanks be given to the Lord, because He has heard my prayer. The Lord is my strength and my safe cover. My heart trusts in Him, and I am helped. So my heart is full of joy. I will thank Him with my song. The Lord is my strength. He is a safe place, my Shepherd who carries me. He forgave the guilt of my sin. He is my hiding place. He keeps me safe from trouble. All around me are His songs of being made free. His loving kindness surrounds me because I put my trust in the Lord. So I will be happy and full of joy for I have been right with God!

A WINTER SONG OF
Worship AND *Praise*

Highlight and respond below

INSPIRED BY PSALM 47, 75 & 76

CALL out to God with the voice of joy for He is near. God says, "At the time I have planned, I will bring justice. When the earth quakes and its people live in turmoil, I am the One Who keeps its foundations firm."

____

____

____

Sing praises to God. Sing praises. Sing praises to our King. Sing praises. For God is the King of all the earth. Sing praises with a well-written song. God rules over the nations. God sits on His holy throne. Call out to God with the voice of praise for He is near.

____

____

____

____

I will always proclaim what God has done; I will sing praises to the God of Jacob. I will tell of His wonderful deeds because He stands up to judge and to rescue the oppressed of the earth. I will make my promises to the Lord my God, and I will keep them.

____

____

____

____

____

____

____

Let everyone bring tribute to the Awesome One. People everywhere tell of His wonderful deeds for He is near.God is honored. He is more glorious and majestic than the everlasting mountains. No wonder He is greatly feared! The earth trembles and stands silent before Him. Many leaders will rise and fall but the Lord is forever.

____

____

____

____

____

____

____

Show your happiness, friends! How happy is the one whose wrongdoing is forgiven and whose sin is covered! How happy is the one whose sin the Lord does not hold against them and in whose spirit there is nothing false. For the Lord Most High is to be feared. He is a great King over all the earth. God has gone up with a loud voice and with the sound of a horn.

____

____

____

____

____

____

Sing praises to God. Sing praises. Sing praises to our King. Sing praises. For God is the King of all the earth. Sing praises with a well-written song. God rules over the nations. God sits on His holy throne. Call out to God with a voice of praise for He is near.

____

____

____

____

____

____

I lift up my hands to His holy place. May honor and thanks be given to the Lord, because He has heard my prayer. The Lord is my strength and my safe cover. My heart trusts in Him, and I am helped. So my heart is full of joy. I will thank Him with my song. The Lord is my strength. He is a safe place, my Shepherd who carries me. He forgave the guilt of my sin. He is my hiding place. He keeps me safe from trouble. All around me are His songs of being made free. His loving kindness surrounds me because I put my trust in the Lord. So I will be happy and full of joy for I have been right with God!

Reflection:

As I drove my 7-year-old home from picking up her first pair of glasses, I flashed back 39 years. I remembered looking out the window as my mom drove me home from picking up my first pair of glasses. I was sad and worried about what the kids at school would say. My heart was heavy as I fixed my gaze away from my mom while holding back tears.

I glanced over. Kathryn too was staring out the window. It was cold. We were in the dead of winter and it had snowed a lot. What was her heart feeling as she entered this new season of life? I was hurting for her. We sat silently in our own thoughts and finally turned the corner onto our street. I was struggling for words. Suddenly she gasped loudly! "What's wrong!?" I exclaimed. She quieted her voice & whispered, "Mommy, I never knew snow sparkled! It's so beautiful."

What I saw as difficult, she was totally enjoying, viewing the world in whole new ways. If we are to look closely, winter is a time of wonder and sparkles. It made me wonder how true this was during the many difficult times God allowed in my life. He must have prepared glistening moments in trials. I won't miss the next one! I now had the perspective of my little daughter to take the focus off of myself and look for the hidden treasures God places in the winters of life.

John 9:25 — One thing I do know. I was blind but now I see!
– KIM

Personal Growth:

What difficult circumstances distract you? Choose the circumstance that you are experiencing and write how you are feeling within that snowflake.

God's
silence
Broken
relationship
Missed career
opportunity
Personal
insecurities
Relocation to a
new community

Use these snowflakes to express the different emotions felt in the waiting. Write one emotion in each snowflake and describe.

Are you missing the hidden treasures of each day? Pause. Look outside the window of your circumstances and look closely to see the sparkles and wonder of the season. Write what you see in the snowflakes below.

Notes

Notes

Notes

A Winter Prayer of *Petition* and *Blessing*

Inspired By Psalm 88

A Prayer to Jehovah-Keren-Yish'i — Horn of Salvation

An evening prayer

Here I am again on my knees, O Lord, in the midst of my darkest night. As You are the One Who saves me, please listen to my cry. Let my prayer come to You. My soul is filled with troubles. My small world is out of control. These troubles haunt me. My limbs shake with fear. My eyes are weak. I am without strength. Every breath I take appears to be my last. God, You are my last chance of the day. As You are the One Who saves me, please listen to my cry.

I will call to You, O Lord. I will spread out my hands to You. Show Your mercy and favor to me. Allow Your great works to be known in my darkness. As You are the One Who saves me, please listen to my cry.

O Lord, My prayer comes again to You as the morning sun appears before me. I have suffered through the night and I cannot win. O Lord, do not turn away from me. Do not hide Your face from me? You are the God Who saves me.

I will call to You, O Lord. I will spread out my hands to You. Show Your mercy and favor to me. Allow Your great works to be known in my darkness. As You are the One Who saves me, please listen to my cry.

A WINTER PRAYER OF
Petition AND *Blessing*

Highlight and respond below

INSPIRED BY PSALM 88

A Prayer to Jehovah‑Keren‑Yish'i — Horn of Salvation

An evening prayer

HERE I am again on my knees, O Lord, in the midst of my darkest night. As You are the One Who saves me, please listen to my cry. Let my prayer come to You. My soul is filled with troubles. My small world is out of control. These troubles haunt me. My limbs shake with fear. My eyes are weak. I am without strength. Every breath I take appears to be my last. God, You are my last chance of the day. As You are the One Who saves me, please listen to my cry.

____

____

____

____

____

____

____

____

I will call to You, O Lord. I will spread out my hands to You. Show Your mercy and favor to me. Allow Your great works to be known in my darkness. As You are the One Who saves me, please listen to my cry.

____

____

____

____

____

O Lord, My prayer comes again to You as the morning sun appears before me. I have suffered through the night and I cannot win. O Lord, do not turn away from me. Do not hide Your face from me? You are the God Who saves me.

I will call to You, O Lord. I will spread out my hands to You. Show Your mercy and favor to me. Allow Your great works to be known in my darkness. As You are the One Who saves me, please listen to my cry.

Reflection:

"It seems to me that some of us value information over wonder, and noise over silence. And I feel that we need a lot more wonder and a lot more silence in our lives." — FRED ROGERS

"We need to find God and He cannot be found in noise and restlessness. God is the friend of silence." — MOTHER TERESA

Stress Management:

How can you integrate more peace in your life so that you may listen and hear Him? Circle the responses that resonate with you, or fill in your own response.

❄ Eliminating the chatter in your head

❄ Talk to God directly

❄ Listen for God's response

❄ Value silence

❄ Choose to be contented

❄ Find balance

❄ _______________________________________

Prayer Life:

How and when
do you use
prayer?

____

____

____

____

____

Solitude:

Describe the
space that
ushers you into
God's presence.

____

____

____

____

____

Quiet time with God and His Word:

What are you
doing to build
a relationship
with God?

____

____

____

____

____

Notes

Notes

Notes

A Winter Prayer of *Petition* and *Blessing*

Inspired By Psalm 50, 55 & 56

Jehovah–'Izoa Hakaboth — Lord Strong —Mighty.

The Powerful One, God, the Lord, has spoken. And He calls the earth from where the sun rises to where the sun goes down. God shines perfect in beauty. May our God come and not keep quiet.

When I am afraid, I will trust in You for You are my strength. I will praise Your holy Word. I have put my trust in You for You are strong and mighty. I will not be afraid because You give me strength. What can man, alone, do to me?

O God, many have walked on me. All day long they change my words to say what I did not say. They are always thinking of ways to hurt me. Lord, you have seen how many places I have gone. Put my tears in Your bottle.

Listen to my prayer, O God. Do not hide Yourself from what I ask. Hear me and answer me. My thoughts trouble me and I have no peace, because of the voice of those who hate me and the power of the sinful. For they bring trouble upon me and in anger they keep on having bad thoughts against me. My heart is in pain within me. The fears of death have come upon me. I have begun shaking with fear. Fear has power over me. Please show me Your loving kindness.

I know that You are for me, O God. I praise Your holy Word. In You I have put my trust. I will not be afraid. What can man do to me? I am under an agreement with You, O God. I will give You gifts of thanks. For You have set my soul free from death. You have kept my feet from falling so I may walk with You in the light of life.

I would be able to take it if the one who hates me were just putting me to shame. I could hide from her. It is not one who hates me who has put herself up against me. But it is a woman like myself, one who has gone with me, my close friend. We shared together and we walked with the people in Your house.

I will call on You and You will save me. I will cry out and complain in the evening and morning and noon, and You will hear my voice. You will save my soul in peace. You sit on Your throne forever. I will continue to give all my cares to You and You will give me strength. You will never let those who are right with You be shaken. O God, I will trust in You, for You are faithful to give me strength.

A WINTER PRAYER OF
Petition AND *Blessing*

Highlight and respond below

INSPIRED BY PSALM 50, 55 & 56

Jehovah-'Izoa Hakaboth — Lord Strong —Mighty.

____

____

____

____

____

THE Powerful One, God, the Lord, has spoken.

He calls the earth from where the sun rises to where the sun goes down. God shines perfect in beauty. May our God come and not keep quiet.

____

____

____

____

____

When I am afraid, I will trust in You for You are my strength. I will praise Your holy Word. I have put my trust in You for You are strong and mighty. I will not be afraid because You give me strength. What can man, alone, do to me?

____

____

____

____

____

____

____

O God, many have walked on me. All day long they change my words to say what I did not say. They are always thinking of ways to hurt me. Lord, you have seen how many places I have gone. Put my tears in Your bottle.

____

____

____

____

____

____

____

Listen to my prayer, O God. Do not hide Yourself from what I ask. Hear me and answer me. My thoughts trouble me and I have no peace, because of the voice of those who hate me and the power of the sinful. For they bring trouble upon me and in anger they keep on having bad thoughts against me. My heart is in pain within me. The fears of death have come upon me. I have begun shaking with fear. Fear has power over me. Please show me Your loving kindness.

____

____

____

____

____

____

I know that You are for me, O God. I praise Your holy Word. In You I have put my trust. I will not be afraid. What can man do to me? I am under an agreement with You, O God. I will give You gifts of thanks. For You have set my soul free from death. You have kept my feet from falling so I may walk with You in the light of life.

____

____

____

____

____

I would be able to take it if the one who hates me were just putting me to shame. I could hide from her. It is not one who hates me who has put herself up against me. But it is a woman like myself, one who has gone with me, my close friend. We shared together and we walked with the people in Your house.

____

____

____

____

____

____

I will call on You and You will save me. I will cry out and complain in the evening and morning and noon, and You will hear my voice. You will save my soul in peace. You sit on Your throne forever. I will continue to give all my cares to You and You will give me strength. You will never let those who are right with You be shaken. O God, I will trust in You, for You are faithful to give me strength.

____

____

____

____

____

____

____

Reflection:

"Choosing courage over comfort;

Choosing what is right over what is fun, fast or easy and

Choosing to practice our values rather than simply professing them." —BRENE BROWN

Empowerment:

Write down a list of what inspires you to be the change you want to see in the world.

______________________ ______________________

______________________ ______________________

______________________ ______________________

______________________ ______________________

How is your community better because of your presence?

______________________ ______________________

______________________ ______________________

______________________ ______________________

______________________ ______________________

Where have you shown courage over comfort?

______________________ ______________________

______________________ ______________________

______________________ ______________________

______________________ ______________________

Identify one or more areas in your life where you need to choose what is right over what is fun, fast or easy.

Make a list of the areas in your life where you desire to be bold and courageous; where you plan to be unwavering in your values...

In the Winter Prayer inspired by Psalm 50, 55, & 56 above, the psalmist says, " I praise your holy Word. In you I have put my trust. I will not be afraid. " If you also trust your Heavenly Father then how do you plan to move forward boldly unafraid to live out your faith on a daily basis.

Notes

Notes

Notes

Notes

A Winter Song of *Worship* and *Praise*

Inspired By Psalm 138, 144, 145 & 146

Jehovah-Sel'i — Lord my Rock

Praise and thanks be to You, O Lord. You are my rock, my wall of strength and my strong place. You are the One who sets me free and provides a safe covering. You are the One I trust completely. I will sing a new song and give you all of my praise.

Thank you for my life. Even if I walk into trouble, You keep me safe. You put out Your hand against the anger of those who hate me and Your right hand saves me. You do not turn away from me even though my life is like a breath and my days are like a passing shadow. You have promised to finish the work You started in me. Knowing of this promise brings a smile to my face. Thank you for my children. May they mature to full growth in Your love and be like the corner pieces of a great house that cherishes the praise of Your Name. May there be no cry of trouble in their streets. May they experience Your constant presence and peace.

I will sing praises to my God as long as I live, for my family's happiness is in You, and our hope lies in You, O Lord my Rock.

You made the heavens, the earth, the seas and all that is in them. You are faithful forever. You help those who have a bad power over them. You give food to the hungry. You set free those who are in prison. You open the eyes of the blind. You raise up those who are brought down and love those who are right and good. You keep the strangers safe and take care of the children who have no father and the woman whose husband has died. My God, you are so good!

I will sing praises to my God as long as I live. I will sing a new song for my hope lies in You, O Lord my Rock.

You answered me on the day I called. You gave my soul strength. Daily I will bow down toward Your holy house, giving thanks to Your name for Your loving-kindness and Your truth. Thank you, Lord, for meeting all my needs and my desires. You held me when I fell, raised me up and called me to a higher level. You opened Your hand and filled my desire. You are right and good in Your ways.

I will give You thanks with all my heart and give You all of my praise, O Lord my Rock.

You are truly near to all who call on You in truth. You fill the desire of those who fear You. You hear their cry and save them. You take care of all who love You. Thank you for Your goodness, Lord. You are too great for anyone to understand. I will think about Your power and Your great works for You are full of loving-favor and pity, slow to anger and great in loving-kindness. My mouth will give You all of my praise.

Praise and thanks be to You, Lord, my rock, my wall of strength and my strong place.

A Winter Song of
Worship AND *Praise*

Highlight and respond below

Inspired By Psalm 138, 144, 145 & 146

Jehovah-Sel'i — Lord my Rock

____

____

____

____

PRAISE and thanks be to You, O Lord. You are my rock, my wall of strength and my strong place. You are the One who sets me free and provides a safe covering. You are the One I trust completely. I will sing a new song and give you all of my praise.

____

____

____

____

____

Thank you for my life. Even if I walk into trouble, You keep me safe. You put out Your hand against the anger of those who hate me and Your right hand saves me. You do not turn away from me even though my life is like breath and my days are like a passing shadow. You have promised to finish the work You started in me. Knowing of this promise brings a smile to my face. Thank you for my children. May they mature to full growth in Your love and be like the corner pieces of a great house that cherishes the praise of Your Name. May there be no cry of trouble in their streets. May they experience Your constant presence and peace.

I will sing praises to my God as long as I live, for my family's happiness is in You, and our hope lies in You, O Lord my Rock.

You made the heavens, the earth, the seas and all that is in them. You are faithful forever. You help those who have a bad power over them. You give food to the hungry. You set free those who are in prison. You open the eyes of the blind. You raise up those who are brought down and love those who are right and good. You keep the strangers safe and take care of the children who have no father and the woman whose husband has died. My God, you are so good!

I will sing praises to my God as long as I live. I will sing a new song for my hope lies in You, O Lord my Rock.

You answered me on the day I called. You gave my soul strength. Daily I will bow down toward Your holy house, giving thanks to Your name for Your loving-kindness and Your truth. Thank you, Lord, for meeting all my needs and my desires. You held me when I fell, raised me up and called me to a higher level. You opened Your hand and filled my desire. You are right and good in Your ways.

I will give You thanks with all my heart and give You all of my praise, O Lord my Rock.

You are truly near to all who call on You in truth. You fill the desire of those who fear You. You hear their cry and save them. You take care of all who love You. Thank you for Your goodness, Lord. You are too great for anyone to understand. I will think about Your power and Your great works for You are full of loving-favor and pity, slow to anger and great in loving-kindness. My mouth will give You all of my praise.

Praise and thanks be to You, Lord, my rock, my wall of strength and my strong place.

Reflection:

"Nothing can bring a real sense of security into the home except true love." — BILLY GRAHAM

I always felt like I needed to be more or better – a better mom, a better cook, a better wife… just better.

Then Amelia, my oldest child, answered a question during a family game: "What is one thing you can't live without?"

"My mom!" she answered. "Because she is our rock! She is my best friend! She is our everything, and a Dad would be lost!"

It was a true "wow" moment for me. Not only did I realize what an awesome kid she is to share such a powerful compliment; I also realized that the person I am now is enough. I don't have to be influenced by expectations of social media; I don't have to feel jealous of other moms, or compare myself to anyone. My children and my husband love me for who I am – who the Lord wanted me to be. He made me the mom I am today, the wife I am today… I was made for them; I was made to love and support my family as myself, and no one else. - ROSIE

Emotional Expression:

Love by definition from 1 Corinthians 13:

Love...

> *Does not give up.*
>
> *Is kind.*
>
> *Is not jealous.*
>
> *Does not put itself up as being important.*
>
> *Has no pride.*
>
> *Does not do the wrong thing.*
>
> *Never thinks of itself.*
>
> *Does not remember the suffering that comes from being hurt by someone.*
>
> *Does not get angry.*
>
> *Is not happy with sin.*
>
> *Is happy with truth.*
>
> *Takes everything that comes without giving up.*
>
> *Believes all things.*
>
> *Hopes for all things.*
>
> *Keeps on in all things.*
>
> *Never comes to an end.*

Use the words from "love by definition" in 1 Corinthians 13 as inspiration to answer the prompt questions below.

How can you show unconditional love to yourself daily?
Write within the 5 snowflakes.

Where have you fallen short showing unconditional love to yourself and others? Write within the 5 snowflakes.

To the ones in your household, how can you show His unconditional love? Write within the 5 snowflakes.

Share the acts where you are a direct conduit of God's love.
Write within the 5 snowflakes.

Notes

Notes

Notes

A Winter Prayer of *Petition* and *Blessing*

Inspired By Psalm 4, 6, 7, & 141

Jehovah-Magen — Lord the Shield of my help — Deuteronomy 33:29

An Evening Prayer

O Lord my God, in You I have put my trust.

Awaken, my God, and help me for I cannot sleep. Prove what is right. Build me up for I desire to be right with You. For You are right and good and the One who tests both my heart and mind. O Lord, do not speak sharp words or punish me when You are angry. Be kind to me because I am weak and so tired. Heal me for my bones are shaken. My soul is in great suffering.

Return, O Lord. Set my soul free. Save me because of Your loving-kindness.

I am tired of crying inside. All night long my pillow is wet with tears. I flood my bed with them. My eyes have grown weak with sorrow. Lord, You hear the sound of my crying and my desperate plea for help. Receive my prayer, tonight. Answer me, O my God Who is right and good! You have faithfully made a way for me when I needed help. Please grace me with Your kindness and hear my prayer.

You, Oh Lord, set apart the one who is God-like for Yourself.

Hear me when I call. While I am on my bed, may I look into my heart and be quiet. May I feel the light of Your face shine on me. Your presence has filled my heart with happiness and brought peace as I lie down to sleep.

O Lord, You alone keep me safe. For my eyes are turned toward You, O God. In You, I have a safe place.

I call upon You, O Lord. Hurry! Hear my voice when I call to You! May my prayer be like special perfume before You. May the lifting up of my hands be like the evening gift given on the altar in worship. O Lord, put a watch over my mouth. Keep watch over the door of my lips. Do not let my heart turn to any sinful thing. I am kept safe as You save those who are pure in heart.

In the quiet of this night I will give thanks and will sing praise to Your name Most High. For my eyes are toward You, O God. In You, I have a safe place.

Response:

A WINTER PRAYER OF
Petition AND *Blessing*

Highlight and Respond below

INSPIRED BY PSALM 4, 6, 7, & 141

Jehovah-Magen — Lord the Shield of my help - DEUTERONOMY 33:29
An Evening Prayer

____

____

____

____

____

____

O LORD my God, in You I have put my trust.

____

____

____

____

____

Awaken, my God, and help me for I cannot sleep. Prove what is right. Build me up for I desire to be right with You. For You are right and good and the One who tests both my heart and mind. O Lord, do not speak sharp words or punish me when You are angry. Be kind to me because I am weak and so tired. Heal me for my bones are shaken. My soul is in great suffering.

____

____

____

____

Return, O Lord. Set my soul free. Save me because of Your loving-kindness.

____

____

____

I am tired of crying inside. All night long my pillow is wet with tears. I flood my bed with them. My eyes have grown weak with sorrow. Lord, You hear the sound of my crying and my desperate plea for help. Receive my prayer, tonight. Answer me, O my God Who is right and good! You have faithfully made a way for me when I needed help. Please grace me with Your kindness and hear my prayer.

____

____

____

____

You, Oh Lord, set apart the one who is God-like for Yourself.

Hear me when I call. While I am on my bed, may I look into my heart and be quiet. May I feel the light of Your face shine on me. Your presence has filled my heart with happiness and brought peace as I lie down to sleep.

O Lord, You alone keep me safe. For my eyes are turned toward You, O God. In You, I have a safe place.

I call upon You, O Lord. Hurry! Hear my voice when I call to You! May my prayer be like special perfume before You. May the lifting up of my hands be like the evening gift given on the altar in worship. O Lord, put a watch over my mouth. Keep watch over the door of my lips. Do not let my heart turn to any sinful thing. I am kept safe as You save those who are pure in heart.

____

____

____

____

____

____

____

____

____

In the quiet of this night I will give thanks and will sing praise to Your name Most High. For my eyes are toward You, O God. In You, I have a safe place.

____

____

____

____

____

____

Reflection:

"Winter knits her forest with frost, as the wind chimes of dreams lost." — ANGIE WEILAND CROSBY

"Pain, and all that it encases is perhaps the greatest explorer of human life. Pain is no respecter of persons and its boundaries can be both frighteningly limitless and wonderfully illuminating. Could this perhaps explain God's miraculous selection of His wisest of saints? Much like our Savior, many men and women in the Word and beyond endlessly endure torturous pain rather than fleeing from it. It is in the miraculous juxtaposition where pain meets obedience that His will is manicured and accomplished! The passage in Hebrews 5:8 states, 'Son though he was, he learned obedience from what he suffered and, once made perfect, he became the source of eternal salvation for all who obey him.' Could it be that the pain and endless trials we suffer are purposefully interrupted and divinely ordered within the cycle of seasons?" — ELIZABETH

Healing:

As the wind chimes of dreams lost, could it be that the pain you have suffered is purposefully interrupted and divinely ordered within the cycle of seasons?

____

____

____

____

What possible positive outcomes have been borne from painful situations?

____

____

____

____

What are your needs and petitions that are a direct result of dreams lost?

____

____

____

____

Share the pain you have experienced.

____

____

____

____

Write an unmailed letter to the person/persons who hurt you.

____

____

____

____

Hard times cause our focus to turn inward to face those parts of ourselves we might otherwise ignore. God can use suffering then to develop us into better humans who can love and enjoy Him forever.

What truth have you found in the frazzled moments of life? _______________

Have you found purpose? Explain.

____

____

____

____

The adversity we experience can work for our benefit. As you navigate through the mistake, failure, trial or bad decision; it's okay to grant yourself the same grace and patience that you've extended to others.

Share how you will choose to live out your painful experience to lead to a positive outcome?

____

____

____

____

Notes

Notes

Notes

A Winter Prayer of *Petition* and *Blessing*

Inspired By Psalm 115, 140, 142 & 143

*Jehovah-Ma'oz — Lord, my Fortress, my strength and my strong-place,
my safe place in the day of trouble —* Jeremiah 16:19

A Prayer for Help

Hear my prayer, O Lord. Listen when I ask for help. Answer me because You are faithful and right. Do not find me so guilty where there is no forgiveness, for no one living is right and good in Your eyes. This world is cruel and the one who hates me has made it hard for my soul. This torment has crushed my life to the ground and I live in darkness. My spirit is weak and my heart fades.

O Lord, You are faithful, kind and loving. You are my strength. Bring light where there is darkness, heal where I am weak and love where my heart fades. Let my life bring glory and honor to Your name and not to me, O Lord, not to me.

I cry with a loud voice and pray with my voice to You. I talk and complain, telling You all my trouble. When my spirit grows weak within me, You know my path. My enemy has hidden a trap for me in the way where I walk. There is no one who thinks about me. There is no place for me to go to be safe. No one cares about my soul. Bring my soul out of prison, so that I may give thanks to You once again.

O Lord, You are faithful, kind and loving. You are my strength. Bring light where there is darkness, heal where I am weak and love where my heart fades. Let my life bring glory and honor to Your name and not to me, O Lord, not to me.

You are my God. Listen to the voice of my prayers, O Lord. O God the Lord, the strength that saves me, You have covered me with Your grace. Please do not give the sinful what they want. Do not let their plans work, or they will be honored. You are my safe place, my share in the land of the living. Listen to my cry, for I am brought down. Save me from those who make it hard for me, for they are too strong for me. Bring my soul out of prison, so that I may give thanks to Your name. Those who are right and good will gather around me for You will give much to me.

You have been mindful of me, O Lord. I know You will bless me along with those who fear You, both small and great. May You give me more and more as I choose rightness and goodness. I will be thankful, as You are my strength.

O Lord, You bring light where there is darkness, heal all weakness and love where the heart fades. Those who are right will live with You so let my life bring glory and honor to Your name and not to me, O Lord, not to me.

A Winter Prayer of
Petition AND *Blessing*

Highlight and Respond below

INSPIRED BY PSALM 115, 140,142 & 143

Jehovah-Ma'oz — Lord, my Fortress, my strength and my strong-place, my safe place in the day of trouble — JEREMIAH 16:19
A Prayer for Help

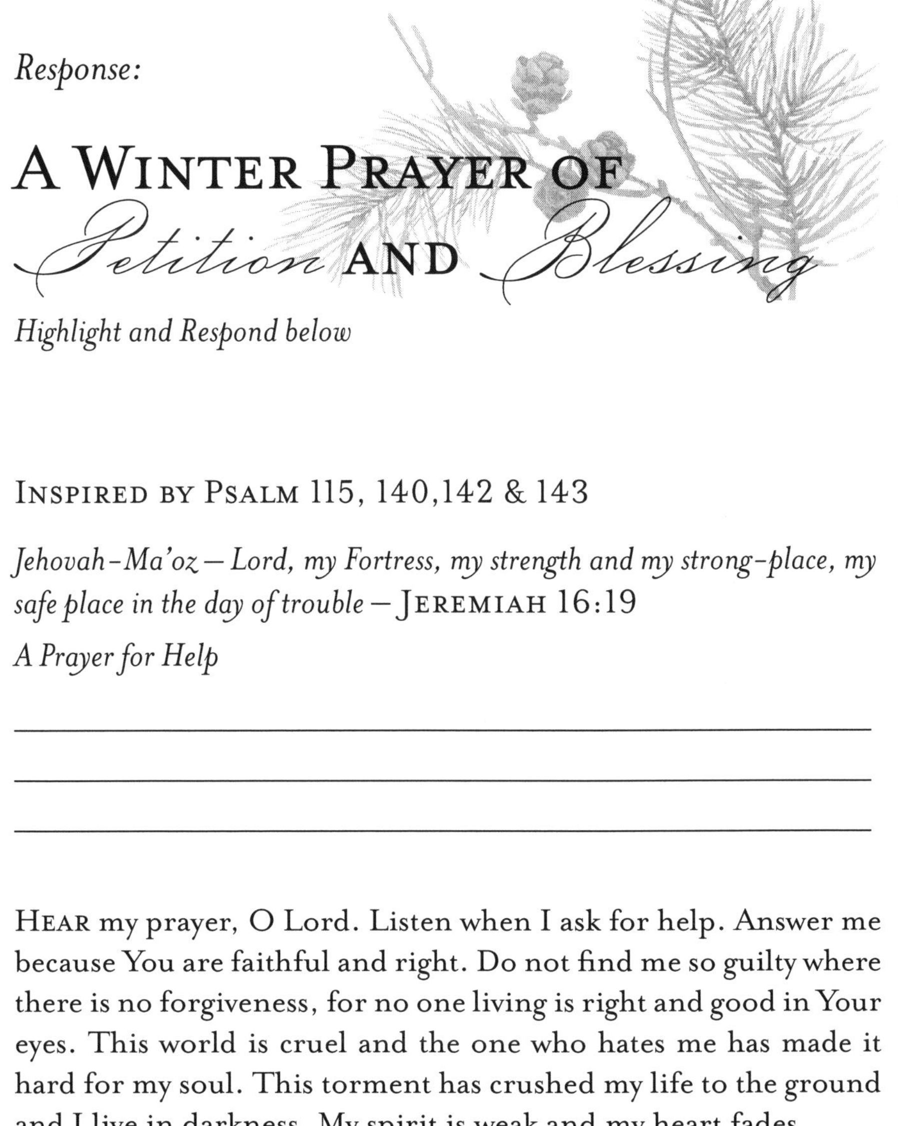

HEAR my prayer, O Lord. Listen when I ask for help. Answer me because You are faithful and right. Do not find me so guilty where there is no forgiveness, for no one living is right and good in Your eyes. This world is cruel and the one who hates me has made it hard for my soul. This torment has crushed my life to the ground and I live in darkness. My spirit is weak and my heart fades.

O Lord, You are faithful, kind and loving. You are my strength. Bring light where there is darkness, heal where I am weak and love where my heart fades. Let my life bring glory and honor to Your name and not to me, O Lord, not to me.

____

____

____

____

I cry with a loud voice and pray with my voice to You. I talk and complain, telling You all my trouble. When my spirit grows weak within me, You know my path. My enemy has hidden a trap for me in the way where I walk. There is no one who thinks about me. There is no place for me to go to be safe. No one cares about my soul. Bring my soul out of prison, so that I may give thanks to You once again.

____

____

____

____

O Lord, You are faithful, kind and loving. You are my strength. Bring light where there is darkness, heal where I am weak and love where my heart fades. Let my life bring glory and honor to Your name and not to me, O Lord, not to me.

____

____

____

You are my God. Listen to the voice of my prayers, O Lord. O God the Lord, the strength that saves me, You have covered me with Your grace. Please do not give the sinful what they want. Do not let their plans work, or they will be honored. You are my safe place, my share in the land of the living. Listen to my cry, for I am brought down. Save me from those who make it hard for me, for they are too strong for me. Bring my soul out of prison, so that I may give thanks to Your name. Those who are right and good will gather around me for You will give much to me.

____

____

____

____

____

____

You have been mindful of me, O Lord. I know You will bless me along with those who fear You, both small and great. May You give me more and more as I choose rightness and goodness. I will be thankful, as You are my strength.

____

____

____

____

____

____

O Lord, You bring light where there is darkness, heal all weakness and love where the heart fades. Those who are right will live with You so let my life bring glory and honor to Your name and not to me, O Lord, not to me.

Reflection:

"Have I experienced happiness with sufficient gratitude? Have I endured loneliness with grace?" — MARY OLIVER

Memory and Cognition:

Take a moment to reflect on the good things in your life and note occasions when you experienced happiness at any scale.

_______________________________ _______________________________

_______________________________ _______________________________

_______________________________ _______________________________

During times of happiness were you intentionally aware of how blessed you are? Many times we take for granted the goodness of God and the happiness we experience. Take time and express your gratitude.

Reflect and note occasions you've experienced loneliness.

_______________________________ _______________________________

_______________________________ _______________________________

_______________________________ _______________________________

How did you cope with loneliness? Did you endure it with grace?
Or, was it a time you struggled with bitterness, finding yourself complaining and feeling life had treated you unfairly? Share your experience.

____

____

____

____

____

____

When you have endured loneliness – the lack of connection and intimacy – have you graciously responded by truly appreciating the beauty of others in a new way? Share your thoughts.

____

____

____

____

____

Notes

Notes

Notes

Notes

MARY'S SONG OF *Thanks*

I am the Lord's servant, and I am willing to do whatever He wants. May everything you said come true according to your word.

My heart sings with thanks for my Lord. And my spirit is happy in God, my Savior.

The Lord has looked on me, His servant-girl and one who is not important. But from now on all generations will call me blessed. He Who is powerful has done great things for me. His name is holy.

The mercy and loving-kindness of the Lord are given to the people of all times who honor Him.

He has done powerful work with His arm. He has divided from each other those who have pride in their hearts.

He has taken rulers down from their thrones. He has put those who are in a place that is not important to a place that is important.

He has filled those who are hungry with good things. He has sent the rich people away with nothing.

He has helped Israel His servant. This was done to remember His mercy and loving-kindness.

He promised He would do this to our early fathers and to Abraham and to his family forever."

MARY'S SONG OF  *Thanks*

Highlight and Respond below

LUKE 1:38, 46-55

I AM the Lord's servant, and I am willing to do whatever He wants. May everything you said come true according to your word.

____

____

____

My heart sings with thanks for my Lord. And my spirit is happy in God, my Savior.

____

____

____

The Lord has looked on me, His servant-girl and one who is not important. But from now on all generations will call me blessed. He Who is powerful has done great things for me. His name is holy.

____

____

____

The loving-kindness of the Lord is given to the people of all times who honor Him.

He has done powerful work with His arm. He has divided from each other those who have pride in their hearts.

He has taken rulers down from their thrones. He has put those who are in a place that is not important to a place that is important.

He has filled those who are hungry with good things. He has sent the rich people away with nothing.

He has helped Israel His servant. This was done to remember His loving-kindness.

He promised He would do this to our early fathers and to Abraham and to his family forever."

Reflection:

"You are currently living at least one of the prayers you used to pray." — TOBY MAC

Gratitude:

In the snowflakes below, describe your gratitude for God's perfect timing, perfect love, ever presence and answered prayers in your life.

Notes

Notes

Notes

TIME FOR EVERYTHING

There is a time for everything, and a season for every activity
    under the heavens;

a time to be born and a time to die,

a time to plant and a time to uproot,

a time to kill and a time to heal,

a time to tear down and a time to build,

a time to weep and a time to laugh,

a time to mourn and a time to dance,

a time to scatter stones and a time to gather them,

a time to embrace and a time to refrain from embracing,

a time to search and a time to give up,

a time to keep and a time to throw away, a time to tear
    and a time to mend,

a time to be silent and a time to speak,

a time to love and a time to hate,

a time for war and a time for peace.

— ECCLESIASTES 3:1-8

ACKNOWLEDGEMENTS

I AM especially grateful to those wonderful friends who shared their stories and sentiments "In the Waiting" that brought incredible insight and passion to this project. Thank you to Carol, Elizabeth, Ellie, Katy, Kim, Mary Kathleen, Nancy, Pam and Rosie.

My thanks also goes to my family for their encouragement, involvement and support. A special love goes to my littles who call me Nana; I treasure our time together and have inserted every lesson learned into this project. And to my husband, Paul: You always believe in me. Thank you.

TO CONTACT THE AUTHOR

Bonnie Liabenow is a passionate, committed, faith – driven woman. She is dedicated to providing encouragement in words of faith to women of all ages during all seasons of their lives. She has counseled women across the country in personal goal-setting, goal acquisition, and time management. Bonnie has also demonstrated a commitment to service, hard work and excellence through her professional career. In addition to serving her community as an author and teacher, she is also the Vice President of Core Communications International , and has been recognized as a successful 'Lady Farmer' by various reputable publications for her strides and best practices in the Christmas Tree farming industry. Prior to launching her professional career, she finished two years of biblical studies at Bethel College, and earned a bachelor of science degree in recreational therapy at Michigan State University. Bonnie is a proud wife, mother of three sons / two daughter-in-laws and finds complete joy in being 'Nana' to her six grandchildren.

Bonnie Liabenow is an inspirational speaker/life coach who delivers a powerful emotional message to women of faith. Invite Bonnie to lead your group to live intentionally, and to experience a new day with purpose and fulfillment.

Contact Bonnie at bliabenow@live.com
or at facebook.com/bonnieliabenow